For the American crocodiles.
With thanks to crocodile specialists Paul Moler and Frank Mazzotti for their help.
J. L.

Dedicated to the preservation of these ancient reptiles.
Special thanks to Jennifer Huber and the Flamingo Lodge for providing advice, boats, and accommodations.
P. M.

First edition 2001

Library of Congress Cataloging-in-Publication Data

London, Jonathan, date.
Crocodile : disappearing dragon / Jonathan London ; illustrated by Paul Morin. — 1st ed.
p. cm.
Summary: Life in a southern mangrove swamp is not easy for a crocodile as she mates, lays her eggs,
helps her hatched babies begin their precarious lives, and then escapes being shot by a hunter.
ISBN 1-56402-634-5
1. Crocodiles — Juvenile fiction. [1. Crocodiles — Fiction.] I. Morin, Paul, date, ill. II. Title.
PZ10.3L8534 Cr 2001
[E] — dc21   00-037962

2 4 6 8 10 9 7 5 3 1

Printed in Italy

This book was typeset in Tempus Sans.
The illustrations were done in oils.
The artwork was photographed by Fred Hunsberger.

Candlewick Press
2067 Massachusetts Avenue
Cambridge, Massachusetts 02140

visit us at www.candlewick.com

CROCODILE

DISAPPEARING DRAGON

Jonathan London illustrated by Paul Morin

CANDLEWICK PRESS
CAMBRIDGE, MASSACHUSETTS

It is deep night.

A powerful light sweeps
across a lone crocodile.
She slips silently underwater.
The sweeping light stops.

But nothing's there,
just a ripple of stars.

Dawn breaks,
and crocodile's world
warms quickly.

She crawls ashore
to draw in heat,
and basks in the sun,
in the sand,
in her salty
mangrove swamp,
by the sea.

It is almost spring.
It is that time of year
when crocodiles
come together to mate.

In the late afternoon,
in the mouth of a shallow creek,
crocodile twines
with a huge male,
then separates
and goes her own way.

Hungry now, she hunts
in the soft evening breeze
blowing in from the sea.

A big buck
slaps through the shallows.

Crocodile slides into the water
and glides between
the arched roots
of the mangrove trees
in silence.

But the deer bounds away,
and tonight
crocodile must settle for
blue crabs, land crabs,
and a crunchy turtle or two.

Yet her belly grows fat
from more than food —
for in early May it is time.

Digging, digging,
crocodile scoops her nest
in the sand
and lays ten . . . twenty . . .
thirty . . . forty eggs.
Quick, quick,
she must bury her treasure!

She hovers near
to protect her eggs
against rooting pigs
and creeping raccoons.

And by midsummer,
the eggs crack open,
one by one,
and snouts poke out.

Digging, digging,
crocodile scoops out
her grunting hatchlings
and gently nudges them,
then carries them tenderly,
in her mouth, to the water.

Now they are on their own.
They swim, and hunt
for shrimps and snakes,
small fish and spiders . . .

and are hunted.

A blue heron leans forward,
freezes — then its beak
thrusts like a spear.

A blue crab scuttles,
pincers clacking,
attacking the hatchlings.

An osprey crashes, talons first.

Maybe five hatchlings
will survive.

But for crocodile
there's an even greater danger.

As the crescent moon hangs low
above the mangrove trees,
the powerful light comes again.

Night birds screech.
Creatures clamor.

Then all grows quiet.
Still.

The sweeping light stops.
Crocodile's leathery scales glisten
and her eyes burn like flames.

The man behind the light
aims . . . and fires!
The night cracks open,
and birds explode from the trees.

Crocodile slides under the water.

The man climbs out of his boat
and wades in.

But crocodile is alive!
Her great tail thrashes.
Her powerful jaws SNAP!

The man crashes
through the night,
back to his boat . . .
and is gone.

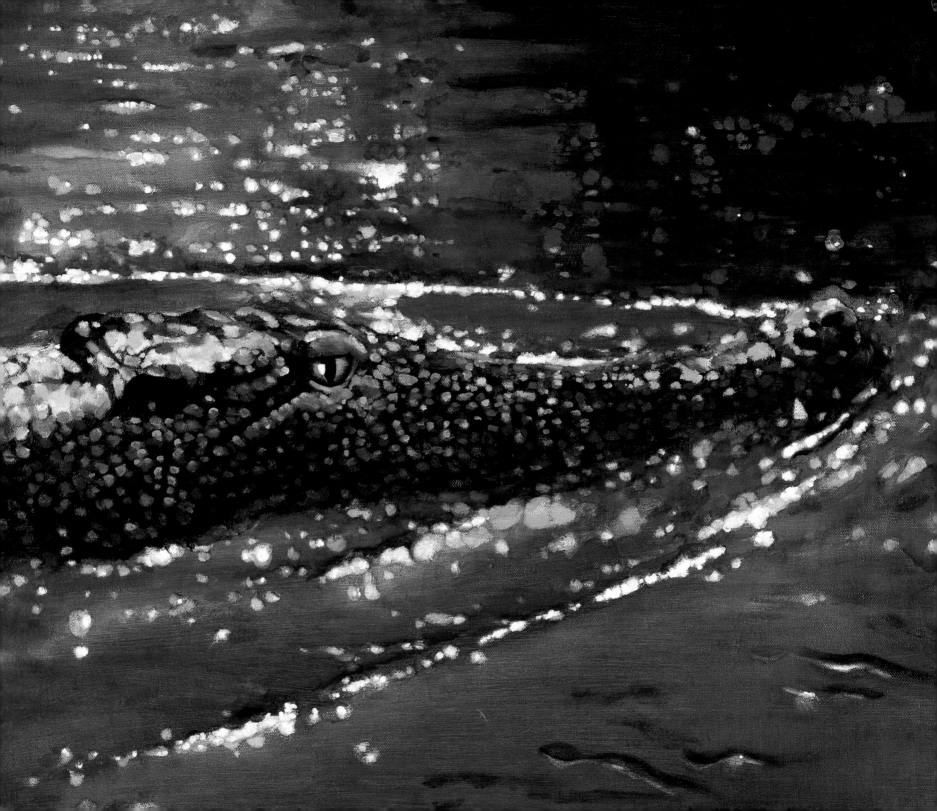

The night sounds settle.
Crocodile swims toward shore,
her ripples spreading
like wings in the moonlight.
For now, crocodile is safe.

And next year
she will return
to her nesting place . . .

and lay forty precious eggs
in the warm sand.

SOUTHERN FLORIDA

LAKE OKEECHOBEE

THE EVERGLADES

U.S.A.

Crocodiles, the largest of the reptiles, build nests and care for their young with surprising attentiveness. About a month after mating, in late April or early May, female American crocodiles (*Crocodylus acutus*) search for sandy banks in which to lay their eggs, or return to the same nesting spots used in previous years. After laying twenty to eighty eggs, the mother crocodile guards them fiercely, attacking any animal that comes close. In late July or early August, the eggs hatch and tiny, perfectly formed crocodiles emerge. The mother hovers near to keep them safe from predators and may gently carry her babies in her mouth, one or two at a time, from the nest to the water.

Crocodiles have changed little in the last 65 million years. What has changed are their numbers. Having survived since the time of dinosaurs, within the last hundred years crocodiles have been brought to the brink of extinction by hunting and loss of habitat. Perhaps 400 to 500 American crocodiles remain in the mangrove swamps and canals on the southern tip of Florida. Shy and reclusive, crocodiles are more sensitive to changes in their environment than their populous cousins, the alligators. Without our protection, American crocodiles may, like their ancestors the dinosaurs, disappear forever.

dream?

If this is a dream, I thought, *then I can fly.*
Up, I thought, *up*, and to my surprise,
the second I thought it, we started to rise!

I could fly. I was free. It was all just a dream!
It was all just a dream,
and the dreamer was . . .

being chased through the air by a bunch of bad beasts.
So I plucked up my courage and said the word,

"Poof!"

"I'd like you to meet my bodyguard, Ben.
Ben will defend me. Ben is my friend."

"RRRRRR!"

That stopped those beasties
dead in their tracks,
which gave me a moment
to go over the facts:

This isn't real. This is a dream.
This is a dream and the dreamer is . . .

me!

That's when I saw them just as they were,
with their rickety scales and their matted-up fur.
They needed attention, direction, and space!
One needed the tears wiped off of its face.

"Let's make a movie!" I said from my chair.
I called out for costumes and makeup and hair.
"But let me make one thing perfectly clear:
I am the one who's the boss around here!
I'm the director. You are the cast.
You must do what I say, and you must do it FAST!"

The wardrobe department
brought costumes on racks.
Craft services came with
mountains of snacks.
We polished their pinchers
and powdered their snouts,
put wigs on their heads
and smiles on their pouts.

They loved the attention, the action, the lights!
I made them dance dances, sing songs, and fake fights.

They chewed on the scenery, they messed up their lines,
but I have to admit they really did try.

At the premiere of the movie
we gave each beast a prize.

They were so proud and so happy,
they had tears in their eyes.

Then we threw them a party.
It was the best!
They took so many selfies,
they just *had* to rest.

After jamming some jammies
over their heads,
I wished them sweet dreams
and tucked them in bed.

Aside from some snoring
there was barely a peep.

It's not always easy to get a decent night's sleep.